301.4

X White $8.00

AUTHOR

Disabled People

TITLE

DATE DUE	BORROWER'S NAME	ROOM NUMBER

301.4
White
Disabled People

THANK YOU FOR RE-TURNING YOUR BOOKS ON TIME!

The author, Peter White, is the presenter of several British radio and television programs about disability.

Designed and produced by
Aladdin Books Ltd
70 Old Compton Street
London W1

*First published in the
United States in 1989 by*
Gloucester Press
387 Park Avenue South
New York, NY 10016

ISBN 0-531-17146-9

Library of Congress Catalog
Card Number: 88-83085

Printed in Belgium

All the photographs in this book have been obtained from photographic agencies or organizations working with disabled people.

Contents

UNDERSTANDING SOCIAL ISSUES

DISABLED PEOPLE

Peter White

GLOUCESTER PRESS
New York : London : Toronto : Sydney

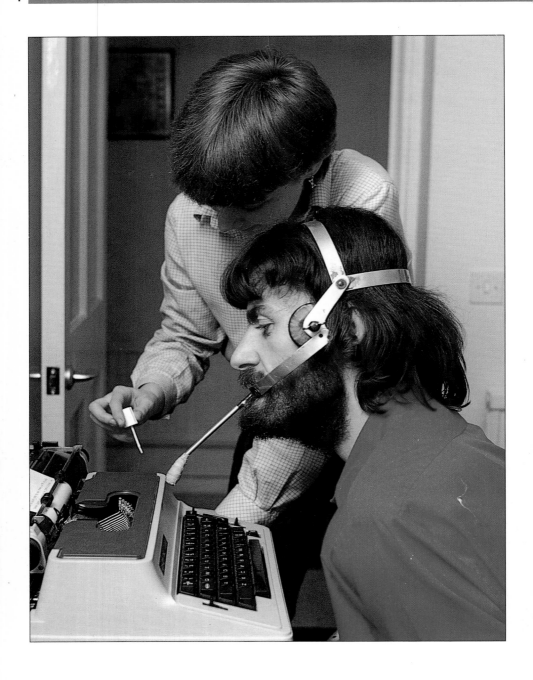

One of the reasons that we use words like "weird" and "abnormal" about disability is that we assume that it's rare. And yet according to recent estimates, one in four families worldwide has a disabled member while a recent United Nations survey says that one in ten of us has a disability. That suggests that everyone must know quite a lot of disabled people. The problem is that disability is rather like a fault. We recognize everyone's – except our own.

In this book we'll be suggesting that having a body which doesn't conform to some imaginary "normal" standard may well create inconveniencies, but it doesn't make you "weird." And some of those inconveniences stem directly from society's inability to cope with disability and from its desire to stress how different, rather than how similar, disabled people are to everybody else.

In fact disabled people's aspirations are exactly the same as most people's and all that varies, as with the rest of the population, is our ability to achieve our goals. We want to be understood, we want a good education, a job, loving relationships and, from time to time, like everyone else, help. This book will explore our quest for all of those things, and look at the obstacles which are sometimes in our way. It will also explore the issues of mental handicap and mental illness.

If after you've read this book your first question to or about a disabled person is not "what's wrong with you?" but "what are you interested in?," then you've understood its message.

Disabled people need to be regarded as part of the community rather than as a strange sub-group. Sometimes computer technology can aid independence and communication.

CHAPTER 1

ALL THE THINGS WE'RE NOT

Jumping high and having fun. Beyond the label of disability lies a vast range of different people with both problems and skills. One thing that disabled people are not is a unified group.

It may seem strange to start a book about disability by describing what disability is not. But the way in which people behave towards disabled people is dictated by their ideas about them, and these are often totally wrong.

"Disability is not the problem, I'm not ill"
Perhaps the first idea to clear out of the way is that disabled people are ill. True the disability may well have been caused by an illness or an accident. People in wheelchairs are sometimes there because of spinal injuries suffered in road accidents or playing sports. Deafness can be the result of an infection. Loss of eyesight can follow a bad case of measles. Other disabilities stem from birth injuries or defects. The disability, though, is what you are left with. It becomes a part of your life like having red hair or wearing glasses, so that constant expressions of sympathy can be very irritating.

> **"If I see one more picture of someone in a wheelchair attended by a nurse, I'll scream."**

Another common attitude is to think that the disability is the person. Perhaps it is natural to focus on disability when talking to a disabled person, but surprising as it may seem, most people do not find their disabilities so very fascinating. Indeed, as a blind person myself, I regard it as one of the least interesting things about me. But it is hard to get across that disability is something you solve – not something you are. What you are is something very different and has to do with all sorts of things, like whether you're quiet, or

outgoing, sporty, or intellectual, your tastes in music and books. This is as true for disabled people as for everybody else. Personality and disability are two very different things.

This boy who has partial hearing can lead a full life with his schoolfriends with the help of a hearing aid.

"Do you know where he wants to go?"

Sometimes people assume that people with disabilities are incapable of letting other people know what they need. However, that attitude is at least preferable to the one which assumes that because a person is disabled, he or she is incapable of making decisions about their needs. It is a syndrome to which people in wheelchairs are particularly vulnerable as a succession of shopkeepers, officials and acquaintances talk over their heads to the people they are with. "Would that color suit her?" "Does he take sugar?" There is no logic to this attitude – a physical disability does not deprive you of your mental faculties, and someone who is mentally disabled still has the right to be spoken to directly.

> "The trouble is everyone sees disability as some kind of test which you either pass or fail. Can't I just be borderline?"

"But you're all so brave"

Unfortunately, the alternative to seeing disabled people as subhuman or incapable is often to see them as almost saintly with superhuman qualities which help them to bear the burden of disability. Disabled people are often described with words like "brave," "always cheerful," "wonderful." It is true that dealing with disability takes thought, imagination and determination. But most disabled people will tell you is that it does not take courage to manage a disability, nor is there anything superhuman or mystical about it. What it does take is immense amounts of hard work.

Of course many of our images of disability come from newspapers and television, and the media are very fond of stories to which they can attach the "super cripple" tag. People who waterski despite losing a leg, parties of blind climbers who scale mountains, or deaf girls who become world famous percussionists get a lot of attention from the media. No one would want to deny the achievements of these individuals, the problem is that all the hype helps to hide the fact that disabled people are just an ordinary cross-section of the public with the same mix of abilities and failings as everyone else.

What is disability?

Now that we know what disability is not, perhaps we should establish just what it is. Physically it can have many causes and take many forms. It can be the result of a disease or accident causing varying degrees of paralysis. Spinal cord injuries, for example, can leave a person paralyzed from the neck or waist down – the effect may be less severe depending on where the injury occurs. But there can be many other reasons for someone being in a wheelchair, varying from conditions with which they are born, like spina bifida or cerebral palsy (better known as being spastic), to illnesses which develop later like multiple sclerosis or very severe arthritis.

There are also conditions which cause the loss of a vital sense, like blindness or deafness. These too can have many causes: nerve damage, infection, accidents, and, in the case of older people, just the fact that some organs wear out before any of the others.

Invisible disabilities

Not all disabilities are as obvious as the ones described so far. Heart conditions, for instance, often leave people weak and unable to walk far without pain, while they still look perfectly healthy. And conditions like arthritis vary enormously, making a person nimble one day but unable to move the next. Epilepsy too gives no telltale signs. One of the most dangerous judgements to make about someone with an invisible disability , and one which is frequently offered in ignorance, is that they use their illness to "get out of work," or they "fake it to gain sympathy." Very few people would put up with the restrictions of disability for fun.

> **"She's not disabled, she'd get up those steps quickly enough if there was a ten dollar bill lying at the top."**

Mental illness and mental handicap

Finally there are the conditions which damage a person's ability to reason. There is much confusion about the difference between the terms "mental illness" and "mental handicap," and no easy distinction is possible. But basically mental handicap is a situation where, due to some malfunction, normal learning, memory and reasoning have been arrested. In this situation the help a person needs is not treatment for an illness but therapy. Mental illness, on the other hand, is a situation where someone who has been leading a normal life develops an illness which causes them to behave in unpredictable and perhaps irrational ways. These conditions can often be controlled or reversed by drugs, psychoanalysis, psychotherapy, or other kinds of psychiatric treatment. It is worth making the point that because someone is behaving in ways which may appear odd, it does not mean they are unaware of the way in which they are being treated. Sometimes odd behavior is mistakenly taken to mean that the person has no feelings. Most of the observations about physically disabled people hold good for mentally disabled people as well.

"You just get on with it"

The range of disabilities just described should make it clear that it is meaningless to say "I understand disabled people." People's individual interests and personalities take them beyond this kind of group identity. However, it is possible to say that disabled people have some concerns in common. They need to be considered when houses (particularly when they are going to live in them), public buildings, and town centers are planned. They need to know they will not be turned down for a job just because they are disabled. If disabled people have anything in common it is that we spend a lot of our time trying to solve the practical inconveniences caused by our disabilities so that for the rest of the time we can be as unaware of them as possible.

With stimulation many mentally handicapped people, like these children who attend a special school, can be helped to make the most of the abilities they have.

CHAPTER 2

ONE OF THE CROWD

Guide dogs can help a person to manage daily life. But if disabled people are really to become part of daily life – one of the crowd – buildings and a lot of our transport will have to be adapted for their use.

For most disabled people the highest aim is to be regarded in the same way as everybody else but not at the expense of denying their disability. That means going where other people go, using the same facilities that they use. But most facilities have been designed with the average person in mind, and are unsuitable for somebody with special needs.

"We'd like to make buildings accessible but it's just too expensive for such a small number of people."

Wider doorways would suit everybody

Disabled people are increasingly arguing that the kind of things they are asking for would actually suit almost everybody. Wider doorways and less heavy doors, while being a great advantage to people in wheelchairs, would also be a help to parents pushing strollers and people carrying bulky packages. Buses and trains which were easier to board would make life less difficult, not only for people with walking problems, but for elderly people and people struggling with toddlers. Using synthesized speech to announce floors in elevators and having verbal announcements on public transport would certainly be good for blind people, but it would also help the very large number of people who have reading difficulties.

Which school?

The discussion about the provision of special facilities is extremely relevant to the choice of school for a disabled child. Will a special school, one where the facilities are all geared towards the needs of disabled children, or a mainstream school, one where you mix freely with other children, provide the best education and the best preparation for life as an adult?

Historically the schooling of disabled people is a recent phenomenon. Until the last century it was generally assumed that there was little point in educating children with serious disabilities because they would not be able to do anything useful when they grew up anyway. But as education became more organized for everyone, some people, for the first time, gave serious thought to the question of how disabled children could best be taught. The answer most frequently arrived at was to set up special schools which would concentrate on one disability: deaf children, blind children, and children unable to walk would all attend

What right do people with special needs have to insist that society changes its ways to accommodate them? Wheelchair access is becoming more common, but many older builings are still inaccessible.

Do disabled children benefit from going to school with able-bodied children, and vice versa? The evidence is that able-bodied children welcome a disabled child into the classroom.

different schools focusing on their disability.

It is only within the last 25 years in the United States, even more recently in Britain, that people have seriously started to question whether this policy is right.

The case for special schools

It is a scientifically established fact that on the whole children disabled from birth develop more slowly than other children. This is not because they are any less bright but because they are denied some of the stimulation which nudges other children to discover more and more about the world. Deaf children clearly have problems in developing language, blind children remain ignorant of many of the objects around them until they are pointed out. Children who cannot walk are severely hampered in their natural wish to explore

the world about them.

Special schools can compensate for this slower development in two main ways. Firstly they can employ teachers trained in the skills which help children with specific disabilities, skills which improve with experience. And secondly they can gather together, under one roof, special material and equipment appropriate to that group of children. This equipment could include a library of braille books for blind children, radio equipment so that groups of deaf children can be taught together, or equipment designed to help youngsters in wheelchairs develop physically. In a special school scarce and expensive equipment can be used by many children on one site. This is impossible where children are dotted about in ones and twos all over the area.

Set against the advantages of special schools is

If disabled people are right that most of their problems stem from people's attitudes, will contact between disabled and able-bodied children make the next generation grow up more relaxed about disability?

the argument that growing up in an environment where all your friends have the same disability as you is not a good preparation for adult life. Most special schools are boarding schools which means that the pupils lose the chance to build up and maintain friendships with able-bodied children.

> **"I'd like Karen to go to a normal school but not if the price is all the special school equipment she needs."**

The case for mainstream schools

Supporters of sending disabled children to mainstream schools say that there is no justification for segregating one group of children into what amounts to a special school "ghetto." Education is more than just cramming in knowledge – it is learning to live in society as it is. It is also argued that academic opportunities can be better in mainstream schools. Mainstream schools tend to be bigger, offer more subjects, and a wide range of out-of-school activities, which is something disabled children could benefit from enormously. But the doubters still say that a special school is more likely to be able to deal with a disabled child's problems. They think there a danger that disabled children will be overprotected by well-meaning friends in a mainstream school at a time when they should be getting every encouragement to do things for themselves.

Going to a mainstream school helps many disabled children feel just like everyone else. If they can learn about computers like able-bodied friends, they will be equipped to get jobs and manage in the real world.

The best of both worlds

So is it possible to take the best from both systems and put them together? One way to do this is to

form special units for disabled children on the sites of mainstream schools. This allows trained teachers and special equipment to be collected in one place but still gives the children every opportunity to mix freely with able-bodied children. This arrangement has many supporters but its critics say that there is a strong tendency for the children in the unit still to be seen as "different from the rest" and for them to stick together.

> **"I think having a girl in a wheelchair in our class has helped me understand that she's just like us, she just sits down a lot."**

"It must be right to mix"

Most disabled people hope that it will become the normal thing to see disabled people in every school from an early age. However, people fear that education authorities will see intergration as a cheap option and will fail to recognize that placing disabled children in local schools requires huge sums of money. If children are placed in neighborhood schools without adequate resources, many will not receive the education they need, and full integration will not be achieved.

CASE STUDY

When I realized that I would have to go away to school I was very upset. My parents tried to explain that because I couldn't see, this special school could teach me extra things.

At first I hated it but after a while things began to get better. I learned braille and began to enjoy reading. But the thing I liked best was playing games with other children and having a chance to win. Whenever I played with the kids at home it always felt as if they were giving me a chance because they were sorry for me. There were still problems though. Although they didn't say anything, I knew my parents missed me a lot. When I was 14 I got the chance to go to an ordinary school close to home. I wasn't sure about it but I decided to give it a try. At first it was all very strange. The other kids were friendly enough but they seemed shy and awkward with me. As they got more used to me they took my blindness for granted. I've settled down now and people keep asking me which I prefer, special or mainstream school. I don't really know, but the truth is, if you want to be part of the world you have to join it sooner or later.

CHAPTER 3

FIT FOR WORK

Many occupations could easily be carried out by disabled people if the facilities were provided. This teacher works in a mainstream school.

Disabled people have more difficulty finding work than able-bodied people, and have particular difficulties finding jobs that develop their full potential. Figures from both the United States and Britain show that the number of disabled people who are available for work but are unable to find it are increasing. Over the years training opportunities for disabled people have improved, though they are still far from adequate. But the really stubborn problem seems to be persuading employers to abandon their prejudices and to believe that a disabled person can become a valuable part of their company.

"I'd like to take on a disabled person but there just aren't any jobs here that they could do."

The quota system

In Britain since the 1940s it has been law that any company with over 20 employees should have at least three percent of its payroll as disabled people. But everyone, including the government, acknowledges that the system does not work. The main reason is that it is not enforced. There are ways to get around the requirements, and prosecutions are rare. The other legal route to better employment opportunities for people with disabilities, and the one favored in the United States, is one which makes it an offence to discriminate against a person on grounds of disability provided this does not affect their ability to do the job. But how do you prove that person A got the job because he was able-bodied?

Favored occupations

Some people argue that the best way to protect disabled people's rights to a job is to is to give them preference in occupations to which they are particularly well suited. In practice this means that particular jobs – it could be clerical work operating a switchboard or running a stand selling cigarettes – would first be offered to a disabled applicant. This is an example of positive discrimination in favor of disabled people.

Positive encouragement to employers to take on disabled people comes in two main forms. One works on the idea that if someone else, perhaps the government or a charity, pays part of a disabled person's wages when they begin a job, this will encourage the employers to hire him or her. Intially this is cheaper for the employer, and the hope is that once he realizes that he has a good worker he will pay the wages in full. There are dangers with this approach – it can encourage the idea that disabled people can only perform a job if they are being subsidized, and it takes an honest employer to volunteer to pay more for what he is getting cheaply.

"How on earth could I take on a disabled employee with premises like these?"

How will she cope with the stairs?

There is also specific help available to overcome the most common practical excuses for not taking on a perfectly well-qualified disabled worker. There are government grants which enable an employer to install a ramp, adapt the washrooms and even put in an elevator, if it will lead to being able to employ a disabled person. In general, laws are now much tougher about compelling people to make their buildings accessible to disabled people, especially in the United States.

Help is also offered directly to the person seeking a job. Grants are available for the whole or part of the cost of equipment which will make it possible for a disabled person to take on employment. For someone lacking power in their hands, an electric typewriter may be essential. A close-circuit television system which will magnify print for someone with only partial sight is extremely helpful. Computer equipment which enables a deaf person to use a special telephone exchange so that he can talk to hearing colleagues is another example of the use of equipment which may help a person function better in a job.

> **"I'm fed up with rejections for jobs without even an interview so now I don't even say I'm disabled when I apply for jobs."**

"It's up to me to sell myself"

But in spite of all the grants and laws, disabled people know that it is up to them to sell themselves if they want the job. You have to talk your way in before you get the chance to prove yourself on the job. Research shows that faced with two equally qualified job applicants, one disabled and one not, many employers will not even interview the disabled job-seeker. But once a person has a job, people stop thinking of them as just disabled. If you are employed, people stop saying "you know

This office has been designed for wheelchair access. Excuses such as "the washrooms are unsuitable" are often given for not employing disabled people, despite grants being available to adapt facilities.

Bob, the guy in the wheelchair," instead they say "you know Bob, the guy who works for IBM."

You have to be better than everybody else"

Some disabled people put themselves under strain by feeling they have to prove themselves at all times – perhaps by not taking a day off when they feel ill, or by working late because they imagine they are working slower than everyone else. This may explain why employers who were reluctant to take on a disabled employee at first, subsequently ask for one specifically. They often discover they are getting more than their money's worth.

Would positive discrimination work?

Some people think that the way to ease the employment problems of disabled people is to have tougher laws which discriminate in their favor. The law has been already been used in this way to increase the opportunities of women and black people. Supporters of this tactic argue that employers will not change their attitudes or prejudices unless they are forced by law to give disabled people a chance.

The legal approach?

In the United States the government has tried to secure employment for disabled people by passing laws to stop discrimination. In 1973, the Rehabilitation Act forbade any employer receiving United States government money to turn down an applicant on the grounds of disability. It is very difficult to measure the success of such legislation because the great majority of employers are private and

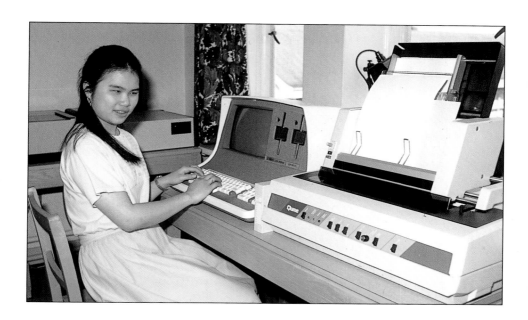

receive no federal funding. The fact is that unemployment among disabled people in the United States is still high – many claim it is running at close to 70 percent.

Britain has largely rejected the idea of outlawing discrimination by legislation. The one law which imposed a quota system on firms over a certain size is, as we have seen, largely ignored. Successive governments have said that they prefer to use education, persuasion, and grants to provide more jobs for disabled people.

Disabled people do want jobs – a job is regarded as a measure of how well you have coped with life. But perhaps now that we suspect that full employment for everyone is a thing of the past, we should also accept that there are other, maybe better ways, of measuring success than how you earn your living.

Disabled people work in just about every type of job: manual, secretarial (like this blind woman), in the professions, running companies, as members of Congress, pop stars . . .

CHAPTER 4

FINDING A PARTNER

Loneliness can be a very real problem for many disabled pople who don't believe they can find a loving relationship. But this woman, unfettered by her disability caused by the drug thalidomide, is celebrating her wedding.

Disabled people are no different from anyone else in wanting to form relationships with members of the opposite sex. Nor are they any different from a great many people in finding the early stages of the process awkward and sometimes embarrassing. Many of the problems that teenagers face when they so badly want to impress a boy or girl come from having a poor image of themselves. It is often based on just one physical characteristic which they exaggerate out of all proportion: pimples, fat legs, or greasy hair are seen as the major hurdles to meeting the partner of one's dreams. The big problem for disabled people is that they *do* have physical characteristics which other people find odd and upsetting. They have been all too aware since childhood of people's reactions of sympathy, embarrassment, and sometimes revulsion towards their disability.

> **"I just assumed nobody would want to go out with someone in a wheelchair. It never occurred to me I might have something to offer."**

"How can I meet girls anyway?"

There is the added difficulty that the physical disability itself restricts the opportunities for meeting people socially. An evening out with your friends is far more of a major operation if you are in a wheelchair. No chance of catching the eye of someone you like across a crowded room if you are blind, or falling ever so casually into conversation with them if you are deaf. Disability limits your ability to act on impulse.

Believing in yourself

There are solutions to these problems but it would not be honest or fair to suggest that they are easy. I know from my own experience how long it took – is still taking – to approach a woman thinking, "this is me, not a pair of eyes which don't work very well and therefore move about rather alarmingly; I have things to offer, and shouldn't feel I have to apologize for myself." Friends of one's own age can be an important source of help: a couple of boys helped me to choose clothes which suited me and advised me about colors which they said I looked good in. No one had ever done this before, they didn't think I'd be interested. Friends can also be the best people to tell you when you are doing something which looks odd or unusual, and which might put off or offend other people. This is the kind of information which can often be taken

Youth clubs where people can make friends of their own age and sex are also very important in helping to boost self-image.

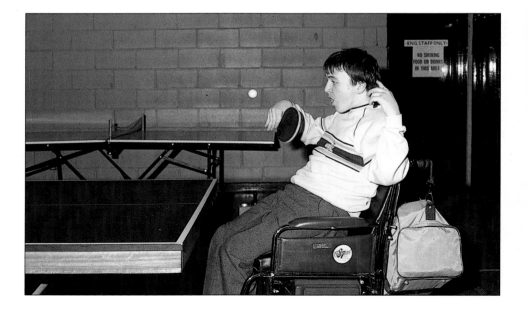

more readily from a friend than from a parent, teacher, or social worker.

"I'll settle for someone in the same boat as me"

The solution many disabled people choose when looking for a boyfriend or girlfriend is to pair off with each other. This often happens naturally anyway. If they attend a special school, or join a club for disabled people, it is obvious that people will begin to pair off. But there is much more to it than that. Disabled people often decide that this is the best chance they have of forming a relationship where their disability is not a major issue, where it will not be a dominant factor in the partnership. For a relationship to work, the argument goes, each partner has to feel that they are putting in an equal amount.

> **"With us both being disabled we both have to pull our weight. Neither of us can accuse the other of trading on our disability."**

"Why would he want to marry me?"

It is also true that people sometimes question the motives of able-bodied people who choose disabled partners. "Why would he get tied up with a cripple? He must be sorry for her, either that or he likes people to be dependent on him," is a familiar speculation about someone's motives. This kind of remark is often unfair and trivial, but it reflects some people's inability to understand how much disabled people can contribute to life – and some disabled people's failure to value themselves fully and positively.

He's not disabled, he's Stevie Wonder. The pop star, who was born blind, is famous the world over. His success shows that disabled people can be self-confident, talented ...and admired.

"When I realized my daughter was serious about Pete I asked her if she knew what she was taking on. I thought he would be utterly dependent on her but he surprised me – now he's qualified as an engineer and earns more than I do."

"I won't have to spell everything out"

There are more positive reasons why disabled people often seek out each other for dating or marriage. Disabled person know when to help and when to leave each other to manage alone, which subjects are sensitive and which they can afford to joke about. Supporters of "disabled partnerships" say that relationships between disabled people have more chance of success because the couple can understand each other better. The truth is there are plenty of insensitive disabled people about and plenty of sensitive able-bodied people.

"I don't want to marry another freak like me"

There is, though, a lot of pressure on young disabled people to try to find a partner who is "normal." The pressure comes from adults, who think it would be "nice" to have someone who they suppose will look after the disabled person, and from the disabled person's friends. Both groups often regard snagging someone from the mainstream world as a status symbol. It is a strange fact that disabled people, though they spend a great deal of time pleading to be seen and treated like everybody else, cannot always manage the acceptance they seek when they are thinking about each

For a long time it was difficult for disabled people in residential homes to marry. But today people living in homes do go out with other men and women, and sometimes the relationships lead to marriage.

other. It is actually quite possible to share society's prejudices even when they are directed against yourself.

But many people genuinely feel that life will not be so dominated by the issue of disability if they have an able-bodied partner. They feel that by getting to know their partner's friends and sharing

their interests they will expand their horizons. And anyway, an able-bodied partner can make the practical things of life simpler – a partner who can drive a car if you are blind, or put up the shelves if you are in a wheelchair, can make life significantly easier.

> **"I used to forget she was blind – to me she was just Angela and I loved her dearly. The problem was trying to get her to believe it."**

Inherited disability

If a disabled couple intend to have children there are pressing reasons why they should consider the issues of their disability very carefully. Certain disabling conditions, such as muscular dystrophy, spina bifida, and some forms of blindness and deafness, can be inherited. This means that a child may be born with the same disability as one or both of the parents. Clearly if both parents have the condition, there is an increased chance of having a disabled child. But if disabled people are aware of the situation, they can seek medical advice and genetic counseling when deciding whether or not to have a child. Decisions like this are never easy, but advances in medicine have removed some of the uncertainty.

Finding the right person

In the end, of course, all thinking and scheming will probably be overtaken by events. People are frequently attracted to someone even though logic says that they should not be!

This couple, who are both deaf, are celebrating the arrival of their first child, who has normal hearing.

CASE STUDY

Ultimately, whether a relationship works or not does not depend on how many working legs or eyes it contains but on how clearly the two participants understand each other – as Susan's story tells.

When I first got interested in boys I swore I'd never go out with another cripple. Stupid isn't it, there I am hating being called a spastic, and then I come out with something like that. Mind you, I didn't really believe I'd find a boyfriend. I mean quite apart from the wheelchair, people with cerebral palsy – that's the proper name for what I've got – find it hard to control their movements, so we twitch quite a lot, and I've got a pretty trembly voice for the same reason.

And then it suddenly happened. I was with our little crowd in the cafe, they were quite good at carting me about with them, when I noticed this guy kept looking at me. Then he came over and offered to buy me a coffee. He wasn't bad looking either. I'd always thought if I ever did get a "normal" boy he'd have warts or something. There was one catch, he was in a "social action" group that visited a local special school. At first I thought he was just doing his homework, but he really seemed to like me.

We started going out together. My friends were really happy, "Susan's got a real boyfriend."

We both were shy of talking about sex but finally he asked "can you – can someone like you actually – do it?" Clearly the social action course had its gaps. But ultimately I knew the attraction was that he was an able-bodied boy – not that he was Dave. In fact, I was forced to admit he was actually rather boring. In the end the relationship finished and I missed him for a while.

Nothing much happened on the boy front for a while after that. Then I did something I'd always avoided until then, I went on an activities weekend with a fifty-fifty mix of disabled and able-bodied. To my amazement I had a great time and I met Tim.

He has cerebral palsy too, more severely than me, his speech is much less clear but he has a great sense of humor.

I took to him straight away. It was a relief to find someone I could joke with and not have to worry if we were offending each other; who understood all the problems; who didn't flinch when you twitched, probably because he was twitching too.

To cut a long story short, we decided to get married. Mum was horrified, she still hasn't got over it really. Friends sadly recalled Dave, but I knew it was right. We've managed to get an adapted house and I am now expecting our first baby.

CHAPTER 5

MENTAL HANDICAP AND MENTAL ILLNESS

As a society we are even further away from making room for mentally disabled people than for physically disabled. Mental hospitals and care in the community are often low priorities in health care spending.

The problems of people with mental disabilities are certainly different from the problems of those whose handicap is purely physical. But the public attitudes which make the problems worse are strikingly similar: a tendency to see the problem rather than the person, and a genuine but damaging fear of getting involved with people who should be "somebody else's responsibility."

"Well of course you feel sorry for them, but they really ought to be in a place where people understand that sort of thing."

Mental handicap or mental illness?

Mental handicap is the result of some form of damage to the brain which restricts the ability to learn. It can be present from birth or it can be caused by a later accident. Medical treatment will make very little difference to the condition, if any, but it is increasingly being realized that teaching, stimulation, and taking an interest, can make an enormous difference in helping mentally handicapped people to achieve their full potential. Mental illness, on the other hand, is like other illnesses – it can happen quite suddenly to any of us however healthy we think we are. It can be caused by a chemical imbalance, an allergy, a virus, or just the stresses of everyday living.

One of the difficulties of explaining mental illness simply is that the causes of conditions like schizophrenia, depression or, anorexia nervosa are still not properly understood. However like most illnesses they can be treated, often controlled, and quite often completely cured. It is fair to say that

while they are sick, mentally ill people are acting "out of character," whereas mentally handicapped people's personalities are partly determined by the damage they have suffered. As this book is about disability the rest of this section will concentrate on mentally handicapped people, but the distinction between the two groups is always important to bear in mind as it is relevant to the way we treat people.

The lives of mentally handicapped people can be greatly enriched by the help of volunteers who have the time and patience to provide stimulation.

Looking after mentally handicapped people

In the past, communities seem to have been able to take their mentally disabled members in their stride. Their behavior may have been a little odd, but everyone had known them from childhood and accepted them as they were. But during the last century the move began to build large mental institutions where it was sincerely believed that mentally disabled people would receive better care and more appropriate attention.

Until fairly recently this idea had gone largely unchallenged. But in the past 20 years, first in the United States and now in Europe, people have begun to question why those who are not really ill should be kept in hospital. This question has even more point when you realize that hospitals for the mentally handicapped are often large and impersonal, and that the communal wards offer the residents little comfort or privacy.

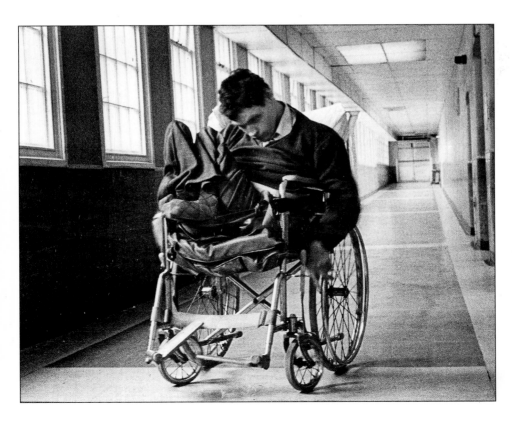

"Throw open the doors"

People also began to question what the right way to treat people with mental disabilities was. As with any disability, the extent of the impairment varies enormously. But large hospitals have not been particularly good at assessing, and then meeting, individual needs. It is being increasingly recognized that almost everyone, however mentally handicapped, has the potential to grow and achieve, but that they need patience and consistent stimulation to do this. Many people have now reached the conclusion that the right place to foster sympathetic help is back in the community, and that the best way to achieve it is to set a target date for closing down all mental hospitals. But the present evidence suggests that closing down mental hospitals too hastily without providing well-thought out, well-funded alternatives in the community can often leave very vulnerable people adrift in an indifferent world.

> **"What bothers me is if we nurses don't look after them, speak up for them, who will – especially once the hospitals close?"**

Just an ordinary place to live

When Sheila came out of a huge psychiatric hospital after 15 years, what she wanted was just "an ordinary home." She got something reasonably close to it – a large house with five other mentally handicapped residents and three live-in staff members. She got the right to choose who else moved in, and to move out herself if she felt like it. She also had to do her share of cooking, shopping,

This man who is in his 20s is severely physically and mentally handicapped. He has spent most of his life in a long stay hospital but, if resources were available, he could be cared for in the community.

and cleaning. She said she felt human for the first time in her life.

> **"It's the first time I've ever lived in a proper house. It's wonderful. Before I always lived in an institution – right from the day I was born."**

On the other side of the same town in a small house lived four teenagers with very severe learning difficulties. There was a one to one ratio of live-in staff. These boys will never be able to live alone. But the people helping them are convinced that their ability to cope with everyday problems has improved remarkably since they left an institution, and they may eventually have sheltered jobs.

Those who want to shut the hospitals say that cases like these prove that anyone can live in the community given the right support. The problem is that these are examples of very good practice where time, money, and staff have not been spared. There are many less thought out projects, and too many cases where people are wandering routelessly from one unsatisfactory accommodation to another with little care or support.

"It's a great idea but not next door to me"

Living in the community means a lot more than staying in an ordinary house in a residential street. It means being a part of that community, being welcomed in the local stores, being able to join local clubs, and not being stared at in restaurants. It means being able to talk to local children without creating a panic, or to make a noise without people fearing violence – in reality, mentally handicapped people are rarely violent.

Unfortunately there are many cases where an attempt to use a house for mentally handicapped people is met by a chorus of protest from the neighbors. While this is still the case it is too optimistic to say that mentally handicapped people have been accepted by the community, even though there have been many improvements in society's ability to care for them.

"It's not that I mind them you know, but it upsets my wife and kids, and then there's the effect on house prices."

The need for asylum

There are also those who say that hospitals have been abandoned too quickly, and that some people's need for asylum has been ignored. They point out that money had already begun to be spent on bringing hospitals up to date, on providing smaller wards, some single rooms, or even separate houses on existing hospital sites. It is argued that these types of improvements should be continued, to provide a more flexible mental health service which can look after people both in hospitals and in the community. The supporters of keeping hospitals open claim that more modern policies ensure the residents have stimulation from outside while remaining in an environment where they could be protected. If community care is really going to work adequately we will all have to change our attitudes and make resources available. Good community care is often more expensive than institutional care.

CHAPTER 6

HOW CAN I HELP?

Helping to arrange outdoor activities is one way in which able-bodied people can help to add variety to disabled people's lives.

Although this book has deliberately concentrated on the many things which disabled people can do, we should not hide the fact that there are times when disabled people do need help. Disabled people are also aware of people's generous impulse to give that help! The problem is that giving the right kind of assistance to a disabled person is sometimes more difficult than it looks.

"I wasn't sure what to do..."

One of the things people most often say about disabled people is "I wasn't quite sure of the best way to help." People with this attitude are actually halfway to being helpful in their approach to disabled people. They are infinitely preferably to the people who are quite sure they know what to do and carry on doing it without any attempt to ask the person they are "helping" if it is the right kind of help. There are some people who drag blind people over roads they have no desire to cross, speak to shopkeepers on behalf of people in wheelchairs when they can speak for themselves perfectly well, and shout at deaf people.

"Do you need any help?"

One simple and direct way of finding out what help – if any – a person needs is to go and ask them. The disabled person will quickly let you know the answer! Disabled people vary in the extent to which they want help. But if you see a blind person waiting by a curb or someone in a wheelchair failing to attract attention in a shop, why not simply go up to them and ask if they need your help?

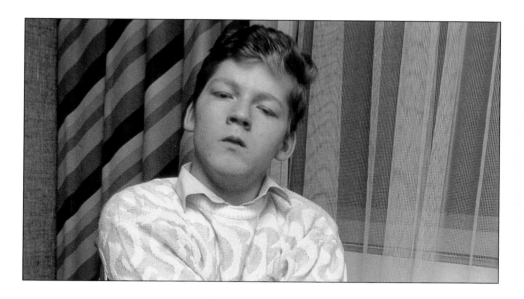

Disabled people know that there are inevitably occasions when they will need help, but that does not mean they have to like it. Most people have worked hard for the independence they have, and it is difficult to accept that there are still times when they have to put the control of their life into the hands of someone else, however briefly. There is a real contradiction between knowing that you need help, yet not wanting to admit that you cannot do something. It is quite possible to find yourself cursing people for helping you one minute and for not helping you the next. Most disabled people have learned to accept help gracefully, but occasionally the halo will slip and rudeness, born of frustration, may follow. If a disabled person is rude to you, there is no earthly reason why you should not be rude back. After all, being justifiably angry at a disabled person is part of treating him or her as normal and capable.

Bristish author Christopher Nolan, disabled from birth, has just won a major book prize for his first novel. His writing shows his great independence of thought and proves that, with the right kind of help, disabled people are capable of many achievements.

> **"Well that's the last time I help a disabled person – he was just so rude, not what you really expect when you offer a helping hand. You can't yell at a cripple, can you?"**

"Is there a right way and a wrong way to help?"
A lot of the fear of approaching disabled people comes from the idea that somehow there is a right way and a wrong way of doing things. It is true that there are different ways of taking blind people's arms, steering and lifting wheelchairs, or speaking to deaf people. But to suggest there is a set of rules for the right way of doing these things is quite wrong. In a helping situation you have two individuals, and the right way is the way which works for both of them.

Just to take one example, the "right" way to guide a blind person depends on many factors, like the respective heights of the two people and the speed at which they want to walk. "Experts" say that you should never push a blind person, but in a crowded train station where two people can't walk abreast the most efficient way is often to maneuver the blind person through the crowd from behind. The key is not what you do but the consultation with which you do it.

In lots of situations disabled people can get along fine, and may find offers of help annoying. Able-bodied people should be prepared to offer help, but realize that sometimes it won't be needed.

"So what has to be done?"
Apart from the everyday casual encounters, are there particular things which need to be done in the community for the person who feels like volunteering? Well, the answer is yes – and often in areas which you wouldn't have expected.

Maybe the standard image of helping disabled people still consists of digging their gardens or making time for endless chats over cups of coffee. There is definitely a place for this kind of thing, particularly as by far the greatest number of disabled people are elderly. But there are also lots of things which the younger volunteer would find more enjoyable. Many disabled people play sport, for instance. There are a great number of activities which can be participated in from a wheelchair: archery, tennis, and a form of basketball are among the most popular sports. Many blind people are interested in athletics, sprinting, and throwing events.

What about learning sign language? There's a chronic shortage of people who know national sign languages for deaf people, and yet the need is enormous. In a whole range of everyday situations, like in stores or government offices or on public transport, deaf people's lives would be much easier if they had translators by their sides.

One of the more demanding jobs which volunteers are being asked to do is to act as attendants to severely disabled people. Some people have such restricted movement that it's only possible for them to live independently if someone can be with them to perform a whole range of tasks. This is demanding, not only physically but mentally. So that the disabled person can still be in charge of their life, the volunteer has to be prepared to help with the most intimate things like bathing and going to the toilet, but also to back off when, for example, they have guests or are working. It is a delicate balancing act and it takes a special kind of

person to get it right. But when it works, the volunteer has enabled someone to live independently with dignity and without the burden of having to feel constantly grateful.

Doing our share

It would be wrong to end this book with an impression of disabled people as a group for whom things have constantly to be done. As should have been clear by now, most people with disabilities are playing a full part in schools, at work, in hobbies and in relationships. We are also doing our share in helping other people: as teachers, leaders, doctors, entertainers and volunteers. Everybody needs help at one time or another; disabled people's needs may be more visible, but in fact we have as much to give as we have to take.

The Olympics for Paraplegics (people immobile from the waist down) is just one of the sporting events for disabled people. Here a victorious team celebrates the fact disabled people can also be winners in life.

SOURCES OF HELP

For further general information on disability, write to or contact:

Arthritis Information Clearinghouse
P.O. Box 9782
Arlington, Virginia 22209
(703) 558-8250

Better Hearing Institute
1430 K Street, N.W.
Suite 700
Washington, D.C. 20005
(202) 638-2848

Epilepsy Foundation of America
4351 Garden City Drive
Landover, Maryland 20785
(301) 459-3700

National Alliance of Blind Students
1211 Connecticut Avenue, N.W.
Washington, D.C. 20036
(202) 833-1251

National Hydrocephalus Foundation
Route 1, Box 210A
River Road
Joliet, Illinois 60436
(815) 467-6548

National Easter Seal Society
2023 W. Ogden Avenue
Chicago, Illinois 60612

Spina Bifida Association of America
343 S. Dearborn Avenue
Suite 317
Chicago, Illinois 60604
(800) 621-3141

The following are toll-free hotlines which offer free medical information:

Cystic Fibrosis Foundation
1-800-FIGHT-CF
in Maryland (301) 951-4422

Dial-A-Hearing Screening Test Information Centre
1-800-222-EARS
in Pennsylvania 1-800-345-3277

Spinal Cord Injury National Hotline
1-800-526-3456

American Speech-Language-Hearing Association
1-800-638-8255
In Alaskia, Hawaii and Maryland, call collect (301) 897-8682

WHAT THE WORDS MEAN

Access the ability of a disabled person to use facilities intended for the public, such as stores, libraries, government offices and public transportation

Cerebral palsy (spasticity) a disability caused by damage to the brain before, during, or shortly after birth. It affects the ability to coordinate movement and speech

Discrimination any action which excludes an individual from an activity (such as a job or joining a club) and which, is based not on their suitability but on prejudiced ideas about the group to which they belong

Epilepsy an illness which involves fits. These occur when electrical impulses miss connections in the brain, causing the equivalent of shorting. The condition can be controlled by drugs

Multiple sclerosis a disorder of the central nervous system which causes a gradual deterioration in the ability to control movements

Muscular dystrophy a general term to describe conditions which involve wasting of the muscles. The best known variety usually affects boys, who rarely live beyond young adulthood

Positive discrimination actions intended to give a specific advantage to a group like disabled people in order to cancel out the discrimination they experience in society

Spina bifida a fault in the spinal column in which one or more vertebrae (bones which make up the backbone) fail to form properly

Index

Photographic Credits:
Cover and pages 31, 32, 40, 43, 55 and 59: Rex Features; pages 4, 9, 10, 17, 18, 19, 21, 35, 47, 52 and 57: Sally and Richard Greenhill; page 6: Arkell/Network; page 14: Frank Lane Agency; page 23: Cole/Network; page 37 Frank Spooner; page 39: Dotan/Network; page 44: Network; page 48: Raissa Page/Format.